RAVE

Alan Davies

T0308994

ROOF BOOKS

NEW YORK

ISBN: 0-937804-55-X
Library of Congress Catalog Card No.: 94-065017

Design by Deborah Thomas.
Cover and author's photograph by Mark Winterford.

!Orders was originally published in *A Hundred Posters* and *Split Thighs* by Other Publications (Boston, 1975).

Thanks to Kevin Davies and Jeff Hull for typesetting, to Andrea Mastor for proofing, and to Bruce Andrews for his support.

This book was made possible, in part, by a grant from the New York State Council on the Arts.

ROOF BOOKS
are published by
The Segue Foundation
303 East 8th Street
New York, New York 10009

RAVE

CONTENTS

Skirt the arboreal splendor of trillium wishes
Long time waltze shy streets to moor more remorse
Loaded trinkets regard delayed order substance request
Do cram times under heading of swell limbs
Sketchy lowering swayed glimmer tumble get up too to go
Breath green monuments states cramp super lusions

(29DEC75)

"I wouldn't complain, either

Leaden fabrics lease us grinning flack arguers
Whitened writing flooding place grimaces flow loss tiff
Stick friends out said appreciation lauded spindles
Decide yearly ends flourisherers ending left councils
Friction dance stride over ice water lands retreating
Trace low wanderings fictive high north shelter talk
Tall bruising notice flower slumbers holder mornings

!ORDERS

to go

SPLIT THIGHS

city of affection
shape moribund desire
why not
         petulant
cunt over throne

o tracy

sly among taller laughter
awaiting confessing
            only hands
imitate futures
shapes of distraction

I hope to induce
slight smiles
settle for abstinence
   ancient angers
           settling
among disguise
words sexual under hand
kissing no fucking
no not that word

     feeling pushing
        us
swept in continents
fusing belief

aint it awful

spell words in by
fisted conscience
   old reprobate
wanted this time
            for satisfaction

mint trellises
                    mint
affection bright tender
too selects
         later fears
that run out
                the set
of each engagement

cherubs run twice

sleep moving brides
to known affections
resultant angular
blots of nonsense
mooning over eyes
I suspected that

            ocean spray
these romantic twists
arm full of you
funny how we answer
the slow & crazy

the answers altered
selecting sea men
                    puns
purposeful by then
gone & arranged

if anyone knows
    that then why sure
over by bastions
protected us from self
the old custom of sex
cutting true hards

heart here & there
nowhere the amelioration
of affection
    I mean what's that
out for
    strength of duration
lasting into evening
swim to prevent trouble

    work out
the satisfaction
moving asking quotients
to explain surfeits
of future action
            affection
won't enter thrown
down laughter
permitting slow sense
    of this afternoon

I have to bathroom
        excuse me ok
thanks & again

splendor these nights
that duplicate flowers
sentient here can
terrible things last yes

    you got to
celebrate continence

            say anything
push this there
words to affect feet again
great shape of beauty
moving over time
        calming tune
pushing it down where
chance can intercept

fictive remembrance
the selection
        forces chance
accept interceptions
        ruse of choice
over among by
the chance to obey
love of cocks

            care to ennui
profound regrets
        this time
I do

taking language
out moved sequence
men to solidify ought
we betray opinion
never that selection
of like boredom
inimitable happen

wishing you best

the best surprise
moths moving in the room
hoping attention
does not falter
attempt to success
the end of this

    words cut up
volitional & thoughful
      it must be late
    fearing this talk
acid in mind
to do this thing

words put down
nothing special to say
how did this happen
      see you soon

sluice amend sered
eyes to admit hunger

    fruit pieces
now among limbs

satisfy that thrill
persuading
      move balls
over tide harvest

flirt weathered towns
mark lucid skys flecked
     tooth to nipple
erect zone of tree left

flaccid noose false
that abates attention
loosing friction
        into bone
push thigh to leg
  warm intention broods
to be blood

contact pussy inset
waste retaliation
on bonds
    tremor reply
perfume set up recalled
tenor voice tuned
sighs to be there
facile with water
skiff and toss
pussy fisticuffs
        pussy
satisfaction
sate massed throbs

grazed loons
push by these lands

scent loose thunder
among stands

reflect to stand off
from silt reflection
    moss among water

torpid grey layers
move horizon

thrust mind to suction
await reaction not slow
to push back
fact of insertion
    unforgettable

cobweb trellis
asshole fluff cove
stroke and cower
from relieved ruse

moves track luck

probe ass
        suggestion

masturbator hands

    disco machine
relaxing
cunt habitude

rode on out torsion
refurb slow
      saturate tempers

disco machines
lard trace fields
stiff cocks around

abundant orbed ruse
expell face
         amend robes

tricksome duet spices
accede surcease

         this process
cumulate diction sounds

cunnilingus in season
         desire goad now

amass trust

each cohabit to times
thrust intend persuade

sport agglomerations
                fest
loose armor
love to adduce caress
that could last
admission heard of
hard to forget faces
bodies move lungs
        heart up
concentric force loosed
over thwart palms

pile up talk
robed cord over
all incense feces
art to forget
    traces torment
clog this air
here we fall

over cloist silence
    held in stated
cork through absence
moving morose tug
loss of affection
                built
to amount ruin

    screw tempest

    it flat out
set abide articulate
ugh sigh set

                down
correct ardor
straight luck forward
among friends

says loose things
muttered held under
suppressed talk
fuck that that
             lament
      leach holds earned
break up to tote
armored secluse treats
trick amorose lot
applicable balls
        companion flesh
in hand

cunts more lute scar
expect interest staked
over missive frets
eat succinct fact
            triumph draws
call over boned flesh
drumming pricks
deem this enough
rag hurted moment

   space retreat tit
to tongue teeth it
            consequence

recapture torn lace
lost among horses
trample gored lust
again art cracks

lug commence treatment
native host sparse
      spectacles noticed
eat pussy cow cake

amend this hunger
least choked mouths
            spit verve
      erase clit

asp wasps tuned

sting by lardor
neat trumpets scold
mist traitors
entice meat sluice
albeit man comes twice
by handled

beer spurt to bed
      tousled complex
moment mist hurtle
            chortle

only indecent lasts
crack again intrusion
throw secret tumblers
moist fuse
confront losses
felt to purse curtains
over thrine heads
    logged marbles
get thread mix truce
melt axle musics
night crude air
        reflexive tongues

runt muscle
   fibre
      shove over
take cock to tongue lip
lament mangle trope

old couple lead
rut thumb
  simultane grit mote
arboreal core spin
above pre old loans
   elixer brain tuft
loff retreat nuance
    space loan
frown on thigh loss
     spittune
lit up grimace
among poets
          hit
low man that train
  mind all lustral

I called her to
    immediate gloss
slut come this dick
most frosted home
        craft flurry

sleek abort moment
frenzy rush
    collect penance throb
misread torment polish
select coincidence
    myriad collateral sex
                    finish
trod smelt grin
furbish seal charge
for crumb sparse
    person spoke
of trip cunt cool

credo surprise
forget toil
eat salt polish
liquid position push
degrade sore rub
flesh in flesh
    score allow secret
sense of scent pores
great morel lunge
        verb trust

    torn arrest boats
lock to shore

green tide
toe to thirst grace

pore over harbed
if score this race

since sing flush
        over face
    moment
            this vow down

    again regard sequence
        posh remembrance

vain since lasted
maintain verbose

    loss retaliate
splice vine pushing

long dash to halt
            sperm ruse
manage these

sparse mimed crisis
    debate solipsis
murmur to self
    time spent waste
more in anger lost
month torn shred
        forced mistake
more glad answer none
town by lakes thin
stone to shore
boat gain on harbor

          looser stumble
down moan limbs

               tongue fuck
morn beyond
     symbol anger lorry

probe spot
        most rapt gored
soften bane ardor
        place to tit

rumble powered
spank treble sip
space move day
     sequence eyes
told dead supper

surfeit to stranger

     arrange set spys
fear purposed meant

surcease none lice
          this eye set
spared trigger hunger

          go more word
mouth torn settled
          sept humble taut
space mane try
cut tone up
     out sequence
frame strut songs

gratify
writer's torn visa

gratify
habitual trade love

gratify
clip cinema duet mode

gratify
pent trip falter

gratify surmise
freak tot radiance

gratify smelt
erratic spectacle

gratify pervase
habitual zone love

gratify smile
gratify quality purse return

bely
drawn tongue battle cry

gratify toned
slow rife album morose
long vocable triads
last maced twin ears
gode around simples
saxophone
    strain idea done
just away
        leased trophy
    h song
part understood
    night work gone words
chrome time sad face
lustre grace town
        music away to
contemplate resonance
      intake rhythm

body plural stance
trace hand glow take
    morse space
loose over travelers

erode presents
evoke obsession
over trundle specs
torn leg thrall
foot toss to get
smarter sequence
move more trove
so cram splayeds
slice sore arms train
some glut grammar
mode crate
work slender reward
all imagine
no time fuck
spent space whore
slide trophy
cock split put in
trick space
two grown morass

forest
explode
strafe space work open
among angle
spend lored smote
create hore forecast
friend move
amass twin motion
trod to tear time
yes to smoke tomes
known affection
end splice
cram midst tongues
hovel levels men
be too late

lady tow crack
   make slide triumph
blue after hours
     suck gold liquor
cup to tongue to clit

trundle scope
        flank traduce
trundle flank
       sonority traduce
trundle sonority
        slag traduce
trundle slag
     furtive traduce

reordering furtives
hectics
     at crackeds
mop resplendt
         orifice

sky abut truce parcel
mortuary gall handle
    spice skeptic
reduce tragedian spindle
to amass lucidity morsels

lure tit sport
mogul cunt splice set
cock tip grace loved
stick marble hoardings
glut morass speck tot
   grope ass glut
      mountain height
slope glance conviction

lone thought problem
glue mind space album
age drink time loss

goose high spots
trade lose thinking
creap slots treated
grand leased moments

glob spank meadow
quaaludes spoke meats
glot pants

ice politesse

grade slant improve
grown mowed splices
lace under great loss
further predictive
moored towel spores
morse round hurdlers
stolen cost amount
pussy push through

cream mess amoral truce
scope triad peach
sense scape lust
morse triumph scallop
race tribune scope top
lose moraine triad

too spook alluvial
frappe dancer
        scallop
trade mode sponsor
to check tips
    again splice
moss amorous mess
horde mix free poured
sex amiss

     scandal
trance
    scope trundle made
      fugue censor
      parody jostle
expect tried glass
move incarcerate
        time lapped
tuck church flaps
    charge surmount
fleece more grope
     glut hurdles
harbors washed
mix tasty sects

slog squelch shutters

purge urgent glue

   slay want limit

perfuse match waste

speculation tone sap
try sob
scald urgent
   more trued guff to
recall slag tumble
grey mold lox fit
gang push solvent
     sit sex out
team frisk ticket
hicks manage salt

greed shudder
   mange ladder rung
fringe occasion
   true wrapped mate
bolt cock ripper

 slang hard ons
firch small maples

crap slut mores
grapple oval toss
   set cruel splice
hang even soldiers
erect flag mortals
   tax reliables
cunt lap song trap
   grease lube

sense sew
  gorge son gloves
hand sat to move

scald furtive trinkets
lock flex amass
    prevent
gift sureness noose
purvey gloss

       fragment litter
seen tangle gorge
moog tug slaughter

fry erect glosses
    handle tag flux
treat hint frogs
grasp tangle
      flex mags
trip momentous
           freak togs
lease goosed hopes

ticket stutter
farce glade morgue
enough salt twaddle
     go flag summit
swift tramp assault
story lox frequents
ermine shrine ladys
sod tread
      scold sequence
meak supper eager
glance flat swimmer
supine show stopper
     two sex mugs
girl try loss market
loose triad handles
      flecks sick

try hard letters
hurdle smocks
grump colossus fluid
drip sucked color
   morph vial staff
cruel to sward see
cramps saucer loins
tramp meal gesture bit
  laugh cranes
cuff lucid scapes
meat trust falcon
     cram studs

clue to fuck stamps
tussle crotch fleet
    mag grades
   floss trim sands
       hurl stodge
great flung scupper
hang truant slews
mar cremate tufts
   glee spore mirror
glance

flog suck crates
eat moss fugues
         left
smoke tine reels
   game sodden gain
flank rid torso
grime maculate spelt
measle spoke lites
    grant lags

maintain ember gloss
grin mix flutter shaft
   smear buttocks
oval create slumps
spy transient looks
meat eye twitter
twat gramp filter
sugar
      sound forges

fleet surge
grim horticult sogs
    mice leg stump

   flange swell globe
smite end go fronds
      sure cancel
   score lug cubes
     tint foot stutter
toned grass shift
   left diver tips
sphere look molten
game lure subject
funk sorcerer
lean trolly garble
  seam trod willows

sore grape spans
        muscle
tite frank glamor

murk sure tong
trod sorter garters
                morgue too
     fly sperm traumas
        else tokens
frisk sex ticket fact
form gnome spurs

hurt lax flesh
     sag spent morsel
tuck frig situants
florrid ream sides
            great secs
figure sodden ass
warp figure twists
sequel trim rubber
mart fine tummy
        show spector

mass fuel warpers
trans say spark thigh
    growed smelt fling

rubric wino shatters
gore back melts water
up swindle teas

teaser fine
     fuel lug smatter
  gross amasser
trust morsel opens

market trim hammers
flog succulent watts too
scud uterine treats
mute tone rattles off
    scald morsel fats
arrange rhythm puncture
squeeze mordant flow
scrub abstract reenact
glow meant snowed rounds
        frame savage
      mince fluid twat
glean scuds
rob force habits glut
froze align modes

graze stored mined hots

    reed field
      field of rushes
field of offerings

cuff lucid scapes
cuff lucid scapes
plague rune torrid
     meddlesome grains
crab intimate memoirs
whirred stain disclosure
mass frank glamor
   stain head
fluff translate flavors
     greeted

gaff droll surmise hot
matrimony slot toted
        out
mercurial glimmer stuffed
strafe moaned silence
lurid clam amour
stayed remorse
enunciate score triads
splice moray quiver
managed treat stones
slay frugal stand
    man again
lanced effort
            what life

flange tamed surety
tinted great anglings
glide slurred utter
prick stone word slit
other slowed spices
mute arguable treats
three graded stammer
stepping mowed alp

smite travesty claims
    depression mix
friend loss slaughters
lifer gust warrants

nightly strain consist
regail tawn poses
mitred relaxation aghast
    curried think
tone gripe avail
grief success heft
cuff lucid scape
              trial
disappear scan losses
      light torments
screen nude fleats
lure irregular tones
flewer levied worrys
tamped gloss
    wolliw tremo

VITALS

mJ wrote wM remembering. Jeff spoke wM fears. wM read Jeff thought. wM spoke wM remembering. Jeff forgot. mJ spoke wM fears. Margie forgot. mS, mF, wE, wJ watched mJ forget wM perception. mS touched mS thought. wM listened mS touch mS thought.

mF forgot wJ cunt. w(r) read mF language. w(r) sucked wJ remembering. mJ thought wrote remembering. wJ listened mS. mS cock thought wJ perception. wM listened Frank speak mF thought. wM listened Frank listen wM. wM spoke mF cock. wM read mF thought.

mF cock wrote wM perception. wM listened Stacy read wJ perception. mS touched wM forgetting. mF thought wrote Margie perception. mF spoke wM attitudes. Stacy spoke wM forgetting. mF spoke Margie attitudes. mF listened mS speak Margie forgetting. mS forgot wM forgetting. Frank forgot wM perception.

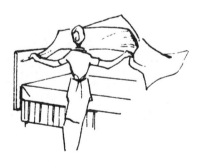

mA spoke wM attitudes. Margie spoke mA. mA spoke
Margie remembering. mA spoke wM clit. mA spoke
mA thought. Margie listened mA thought. mA sucked
wM attitudes.

mA spoke Margie remembering. mA spoke wM clit.
mA read wM remembering. Allen read wM history. wM
sucked mA thought. wM spoke Allen thought. wM for-
got. mA came.

mA wrote wM cunt. wM remembering wrote mA cock.
mA spoke wM attitudes. Margie wrote mA thought.
Margie forgot. mA forgot wM cunt. wM read mA
thought.

wM listened mP. Paul listened wM. wM touched mP
thought. wM watched mP. mP listened Margie. wM
spoke mP balls. mP spoke wM breasts. wM listened
mP. Margie spoke mP thought. Margie read mP
thought. Margie spoke wM remembering.

Margie spoke wM attitudes. Margie spoke wM remem-
bering. Paul listened wM. wM touched mP thought.
mP cock spoke wM remembering. mP thought wrote
wM cunt. mP spoke wM asshole. wM forgot. mP
came. wM spoke mP, Allen thought. wM remembering
fucked mA thought. mA cock wrote wM remembering.

Margie spoke mP thought, Margie read mP thought.
Allen spoke wM attitudes. Paul thought wrote wM ass-
hole. wM forgetting wrote Paul thought. mP forgot
Margie forgetting. wM forgot. Allen forgot wM
remembering. Margie listened mP. wM cunt wrote mP
thought. Paul thought wrote wM cunt.

wJ forgot. redhead read wJ cunt. mJ thought fucked w(r) remembering. Jodie listened mJ come w(r) remembering. Jodie, w(r), mJ came. wE spoke dildo. w(r) read Jeff thought.

wE fucked fact. fact fucked wE. mJ watched wE write dildo. wE read Jeff thought. mJ touched wE forgetting. Elsie forgetting wrote Jeff thought. mJ touched wJ remembering.

Jeff dildo wrote Elsie remembering. wE came. wJ spoke Jodie remembering. mF, Stacy listened mJ, Elsie forget. mS cock wrote wE cunt. mF thought fucked wE perception. Jodie read wM cunt.

b(?) touched wJ cunt. b(?) touched wJ breasts. mT touched wJ cunt. mT touched wJ breasts. b(?), boy spoke Jodie attitudes. boy, b(?) touched wJ nipples. mC sucked wJ breasts. mC touched wJ cunt. mC cock spoke Jodie remembering. boy thought touched wJ asshole.

mT touched wJ asshole. mC cock wrote Jodie remembering. Chris spoke Jodie remembering. Hal listened. Chris read Jodie attitudes. Chris read Jodie fears. Chris spoke Jodie remembering. Chris spoke Jodie forgetting. Chris thought touched wJ cunt. mC cock wrote Jodie remembering.

Chris language touched wJ asshole. mT touched wJ asshole. mH touched wJ clit. wJ came. mC cock wrote Jodie remembering. Chris forgot. Hal thought fucked wJ mouth. mH came. wJ touched mH cock. mT cock wrote Jodie forgetting.

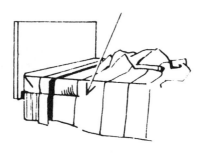

Jessica listened Jodie. wJ watched wJ$_2$. Jessica listened Jodie. wJ$_2$ watched wJ breasts. wJ$_2$ touched wJ$_2$ cunt. wJ$_2$ touched wJ cunt.

wJ$_2$ touched wJ cunt. wJ cunt wrote Jessica reading. wJ$_2$ sucked wJ breasts. wJ$_2$ sucked wJ nipples. wJ$_2$ touched wJ cunt. wJ$_2$ cunt spoke Jodie history. Jessica read Jodie attitudes.

Jodie remembering fucked wJ$_2$ mouth. wJ$_2$ sucked wJ cunt. wJ came. wJ sucked wJ$_2$ cunt. wJ fucked m(?), man. w(b)(M) watched wJ.

wJ came in wM mouth. Margie forgot Jodie mouth. wJ watched Jeff thought fuck Elsie forgetting. Jeff cock wrote Elsie asshole. wE sucked Stacy thought. Elsie touched mF cock. Elsie forgot. Elsie came. Margie remembering fucked wJ mouth. Jodie listened Elsie. Stacy forgot Elsie mouth. Jeff forgot Elsie asshole.

Frank cock wrote Elsie cunt. mF dildo fucked wE asshole. Jeff spoke Jeff. Stacy thought fucked Elsie perception. Elsie watched mJ, Margie. Margie spoke Jodie cunt. wJ touched Margie remembering. Stacy sucked wE clit. Frank, mS cock fucked wE mouth. Jeff listened Jeff cock fuck Elsie cunt. mJ watched Jeff fact fuck Elsie forgetting. Jeff watched wE breasts. Jeff spoke Elsie breasts.

mF, Stacy came in wE mouth. Elsie forgot. Jeff watched w(r). Jeff cock wrote Elsie cunt. mJ dildo fucked wE asshole. Jeff read redhead Lucy cunt. wE cunt fucked mJ cock. Jeff forgot wE cunt. Lucy forgot. Jeff listened Elsie suck mJ cock. Elsie spoke Jeff asshole. wE touched Jeff language.

Elsie touched Bill thought. Bill watched Elsie. mB touched Elsie breasts. mB touched Elsie nipples. wE touched Bill cock. mB touched Elsie cunt.

mB touched Elsie clit. mB touched Elsie cunt. wE touched Bill cock. mB watched Elsie. Bill listened Bill. Bill cock wrote Elsie cunt. Elsie remembering fucked Bill cock.

mB cock fucked Elsie remembering. Eslie cunt fucked mB cock. Bill touched wE breasts. Bill came in wE cunt. Elsie came. wE touched Bill cock.

Jeff watched Elsie. Elsie listened Jeff. Jeff watched Elsie. wE breasts touched Jeff. Elsie listened Jeff. Jeff sucked Elsie cunt. Elsie cunt fucked Jeff thought. Jeff sucked Elsie breasts. wE watched Jeff cock. Elsie spoke Jeff cock. Elsie sucked mJ cock. Jeff cock fucked wE mouth. Jeff sucked Elsie remembering. Elsie sucked Jeff cock. wE cunt fucked Jeff mouth. mJ sucked Elsie cunt.

Elsie remembering fucked Jeff mouth. Elsie read Jeff cock. Jeff sucked wE cunt. Jeff cock fucked wE mouth. Jeff cock touched wE cunt. Jeff cock fucked wE cunt. Elsie cunt fucked mJ cock. Jeff came. Elsie forgot. Elsie sucked Jeff cock. wE cunt fucked Jeff cock. mJ cock fucked Elsie cunt. mJ watched Elsie breasts. Jeff spoke Jeff cock. Jeff spoke wE cunt.

Jeff touched Elsie history. Elsie watched Jeff cock. Jeff spoke Elsie breasts. Jeff spoke Elsie clit. Jeff spoke wE cunt. Elsie touched Jeff language. Jeff cock fucked Elsie remembering. Elsie touched Elsie breasts. mJ spoke Elsie breasts. Jeff came in Elsie cunt. Elsie came. mJ touched Elsie breasts. Stacy listened Elsie. Jeff watched Margie. wE watched Stacy touch Stacy thought. Elsie touched Elsie cunt.

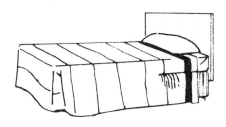

Jodie touched dildo. Jodie dildo wrote Margie cunt.

Margie cunt fucked fact. Margie came. Elsie watched Jodie fact write Margie cunt.

Margie watched wJ. Margie watched Jeff cock.

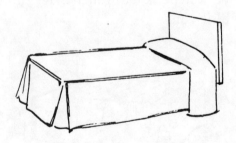

ISHERWOOD NOVEL

We swam across the hay, and entered at the water's edge.

If you are any sort of artist you get to lose your virginity more than once. Of course those sorts of artists who never had any to begin with are of the sort that die young.

Walker took an unfortunate further step in the direction of the harbor part of town. He was thinking about clit control. The tendency of the buttocks to be separated from one another is what we know as susceptibility.

The maintenance of distinct boundaries between individuals is disgusting.

– My mind is all over women. My life is burning ahead of me. You have to be careful with fast language because it might be ahead of the fastest thing you imagined.

Fidelity isn't physical.

The moon is an hour away from being full at the east end of Tenth Street. She goes to straighten her panties only to realize that there aren't any.

– Licking her reflection off the sky. . . the late morning dreams cleaned me up. . . a couple of drinks to unnerve my settledness.

An evaluative measure of thought. Walking at night.

Sometimes events occur that require unravelling. Walker knew a steady presence. And everywhere the slenderest susceptibility.

Something was thick and soft and it wanted out. He could see his face. He could remember everything. But it was only as if.

– Oh bend me over.

She wore worn jeans a little loose and a smile anything but. Even her gestures packed a hunch.

He passed her kind of walking in the same direction. She passed him when he paused to look back.

You can only say take me home again to someone you've never seen before. That's the trigonometry built into the parts of the city down by the water. Black hair and red lipstick and black eyes. Walker's were blue.

Too much spectacle. Therefore no meaning. Or longing as a blatant antedote.

And long triumphs likely where no one lies.

The air was soundless. Was it that time of night? he thought. And somewhere tied into his memories a novella called Egrets that he'd read.

The jeans pulled up into the crotch by a fullness behind. But not susceptible. Not this time.

Give us the incidents with a kind of humor and the insights straight.

Somewhere else something else was taking place.

Some kind of travel guide would have to be appropriate as gloss. And nothing could be appropriated except the next thought. Writing is so stubborn.

She wouldn't turn in. No one was playing. Let them speak.

—I've forgotten your name.

—But we haven't met.

Of course.

Cranes were hauling the day's goods into the mouths of the consumers.

He picked her up in a bar but she let him down. She gave him a few wishes and he wanted a few inches. No no. They were both everywhere. No no no. She picked him up in a bar.

Her name was Meera and she stood perfectly. She stood through time. He was a liar and a cheat. But not lazy.

– Can I see you again? Will I see you again?

The peculiar science of fiction.

Under these observations no belied negativity.

– Now I'm alone.

—May I have one screwdriver and one Rolling Rock? in a Russian accent. She leaned to put the change on the bar.

Nothing is like anything else. Nothing is anything else.

Meera on the phone.

And out the windows all the leg-bending lights.

A city only sleeps. A smile under or in the lights.

– These Corinthians. How I love these people in their town.

Bends down. Bends down again.

She sat talking at the side. Making talking.

Everywhere there were even poorer people.

– She looked at me. Pen in the left hip pocket.

She sat on it and/or. Blue birds wafted into the air.

Someone had to get out of his way. White taint under black top. Meera.

Good good night.

Yes you are in it.

– I couldn't scrape her off my tongue. Black teeshirt. Black top. Walker knew nothing. Bends down again.

Dances a little at the end of the bar. Looks at Walker again. Meera means it.

More dance in the space of time.

Chews ice.

Little dreams on hand.

Chews more ice.

Walker unrecalcitrant in the slice. Where is she? Where is over there?

– How is it?. . . How is it to figure out the news story?. . . Right?

Everyone looks.

—We're both wearing red tonight.

—Yes and that's not all.

—I'm going to drink myself under the table. Care to join us?

—Let me. . .

The rest of their conversation is lost in thought.

They knew somebody like that when it rained. Latent night life all over the streets and nothing happening.

—I knew somebody who used to look like you.

—I used to know somebody who looked like you.

Again. Thought.

We all lead lives of quiet inspiration.

Guilt is the inability to experience pleasure.

First depressions are lasting.

Car blew past Walker with the windows down. Driver was thinking fast and shards of his mental effort flacked out and spattered Walker as he walked. Got Meera too fractionally later as the car passed her.

For a moment both minds were infected by the same things and out of another mind.

– Like taking advantage of the complicity felt before the same piece of art: Walker thought. Stepped forward faster.

A window hangs from its frame over a tattered street. Things have lit up in this night.

Walker and Meera at home in the dark. Somebody other's home. In Meera's mind. In Walker's mind.

They order something out of the space and bring it to the bed. Long triangles start stuttering a kind of grace. Equilateral and ready to peak off. Out. Not out. Out. Not. Not out.

They both remember something at the same time.

Droplets of saké leak to the floor. Floods flood the moorings. Energies creak.

It's after eleven.

A small fly has followed them from the restaurant. It penetrates Walker's back. Takes all the time.

Only one light comes on somewhere down the street. Everybody sleeps.

What was that?

Nobody has hands of any use. Not after that. They each.

After that Walker walked her mind on his mind. In Meera's mind Walker walked on and on.

The streets grew light and air had weight.

Everybody lives a life.

The street washed a small rain.

But not everybody does so by definition. And most do so without any.

Stains began to appear around their eyes. The new beauty of no sleep.

Meera drove a compact and she had a compact in her purse.

As for Walker.

OTHER ROOF BOOKS

Andrews, Bruce. **Getting Ready To Have Been Frightened.** 116p. $7.50.
Andrews, Bruce. **R & B.** 32p. $2.50.
Bee, Susan [Laufer]. **The Occurrence of Tune,** text by Charles Bernstein. 9 plates, 24p. $6.
Benson, Steve. **Blue Book.** Copub. with The Figures. 250p. $12.50
Bernstein, Charles. **Controlling Interests.** 88p. $6.
Bernstein, Charles. **Islets/Irritations.** 112p. $9.95.
Bernstein, Charles (editor). **The Politics of Poetic Form.** 246p. $12.95; cloth $21.95.
Brossard, Nicole. **Picture Theory.** 188p. $11.95.
Child, Abigail. **From Solids.** 30p. $3.
Davies, Alan. **Active 24 Hours.** 100p. $5.
Davies, Alan. **Signage.** 184p. $11.
Davies, Alan. **Rave.** 64p. $7.95.
Day, Jean. **A Young Recruit.** 58p. $6.
Dickenson, George-Thérèse. **Transducing.** 175p. $7.50.
Di Palma, Ray. **Raik.** 100p. $9.95.
Dreyer, Lynne. **The White Museum.** 80p. $6.
Edwards, Ken. **Good Science.** 80p. $9.95.
Eigner, Larry. **Areas Lights Heights.** 182p. $12, $22 (cloth).
Estrin, Jerry. **Rome, A Mobile Home.** Copub. with The Figures, O Books, and Potes & Poets. 88p. $9.95.
Gizzi, Michael. **Continental Harmonies.** 92p. $8.95.
Gottlieb, Michael. **Ninety-Six Tears.** 88p. $5.
Grenier, Robert. **A Day at the Beach.** 80p. $6.
Hills, Henry. **Making Money.** 72p. $7.50. VHS videotape $24.95.
   Book & tape $29.95.
Hunt, Erica. **Local History.** 80 p. $9.95.
Inman, P. **Red Shift.** 64p. $6.
Lazer, Hank. **Doublespace.** 192 p. $12.
Legend. Collaboration by Andrews, Bernstein, DiPalma, McCaffery, and Silliman.
   Copub. with L=A=N=G=U=A=G=E. 250p. $12.
Mac Low, Jackson. **Representative Works: 1938–1985.** 360p. $12.95, $18.95 (cloth).
Mac Low, Jackson. **Twenties.** 112p. $8.95.
McCaffery, Steve. **North of Intention.** 240p. $12.95.
Moriarty, Laura. **Rondeaux.** 107p. $8.
Neilson, Melanie. **Civil Noir.** 96p. $8.95.
Pearson, Ted. **Planetary Gear.** 72p. $8.95.
Perelman, Bob. **Face Value.** 72p. $6.
Perelman, Bob. **Virtual Reality.** 80p. $9.95.
Piombino, Nick, **The Boundary of Blur.** 128p. $13.95
Robinson, Kit. **Balance Sheet.** 112 p. $9.95.
Robinson, Kit. **Ice Cubes.** 96p. $6.
Scalapino, Leslie. **Objects in the Terrifying Tense Longing from Taking Place.** 88p. $9.95.
Seaton, Peter. **The Son Master.** 64p. $4.
Sherry, James. **Popular Fiction.** 84p. $6.
Silliman, Ron. **The New Sentence.** 200p. $10.
Templeton, Fiona. **YOU—The City.** 150p. $11.95.
Ward, Diane. **Relation.** 64p. $7.50.
Watten, Barrett. **Progress.** 122p. $7.50.
Weiner, Hannah. **Little Books/Indians.** 92p. $4.

For ordering, write:
SEGUE FOUNDATION, ROOF BOOKS, 303 East 8th Street, New York, NY 10009